Sane Response

Red Penguin
BOOKS

Sane Response

A JOURNEY THROUGH DIVORCE TO DISCOVERY
SOMETIMES, IT RHYMES

MOLLY SARGENT

Sane Response

Copyright © 2024 by Molly Sargent

All Rights Reserved.

Library of Congress Control Number: 2023923602

No part of this book may be reproduced or used in any manner without the written permission of the copyright owner except for the use of quotations in a book review.

First Edition
Published by Red Penguin Books

Cover image by Gretchen Kelly
Cover design by Denika Dutil and Martine Cameau
Interior design by Denika Dutil and Suzanne Uchytil

ISBN: 978-1-63777-533-2 (digital)
ISBN: 978-1-63777-534-9 (softcover)

This book is printed in the United States of America.

dedication

For women

*If it's true,
just for you,
that's enough.*

and for MaryAnn

my mother

*"A sane person
to an insane society
must appear insane."*

~ Kurt Vonnegut

preface

Dear friend on the journey . . .

I didn't get married thinking I'd get divorced. But eventually, divorce became my calling.

Divorce is a kind of loss; a death; a saying of goodbye—to a partner, money, family, identities (many). It's disruptive and public. And even when it's the healthy option, it can be hard; divorce dismantles dreams.

In the wake of my divorce (and admittedly, in the preamble leading up to it), I discovered feelings that begged to be felt (reluctantly), questions that demanded to be asked (begrudgingly), denials that needed to be challenged (embarrassingly), and truths that hoped to be reconciled (encouragingly).

In the short-term, my divorce resolved many immediate issues, but it also invited new challenges for me to deal with. My first response was to blame him; there was much "evidence" to support the "rightness" of my blame campaign (and wow, did being right feel good!).

But in reality, my blame tactic only served to temporarily (if conveniently) distract me from the real work that lay ahead. It took time, but I came to accept how my relationship was more "a catalyst for change" than "the cause of my pain." And soon enough, the practical aspects of *getting on with my life* demanded that I pivot—away from my publicly-acceptable-but-privately-unhelpful story of victimhood into an inwardly self-supporting story of authorship.

Inevitably, I arrived at the stage of "no longer wife"—the moments of removing my wedding ring for the last time and of checking the "D" box on medical forms—solemn ceremonies conducted in solitude, a stark contrast to the fanfare of wedding whites, bouquets and champagne.

Meanwhile, as the triage responses from friends and family waned (compassion has its expiration date), I was finally compelled to take stock of the narrative of my present and future.

Notably, *that* process required me to retrace—and face—the steps of my past. With no-holds-barred introspection (and skillful counseling), I began facing (and forgiving) any factor from my past—small or large—in the guise of any person, place or event, that brought me to this point in my present.

I learned to turn my attention away from the question, "How did this happen to me?!" and to apply, instead, an uncomfortable curiosity, asking "How might this have happened *by* me or *for* me?" It was these explorations that paved the way for me to ponder, more productively, "What now?" and "What next?"

Quickly (and with support), I saw how "past became prologue"—useful as a reference, but no longer as a refuge! My life's meaning and purpose would need to be redefined and redesigned. To do that, I had to muster the courage to honestly feel-the-feels (even the ugly ones), to unpack their messages, and to apply new thinking that would "unstuck" me from my old stories and beliefs. There were misconceptions, misperceptions, and hurts from my youth to which I could now lovingly lend my adult perspective. And there were revised beliefs (and new boundaries), which I would need to embrace to shift from surviving to thriving.

That was—and remains—the journey.

How this book organized itself . . .

The poems that make up *Sane Response* are organized into five chapters, which serendipitously suggested themselves into an arc of transformation!

You see, I had compiled many poems from my decades of journals, and selected the ones related most closely to my experiences (or just my observations) of love, relationship, connection, marriage, motherhood, and breakup—basically, the primary roles of mom, wife, friend, and woman. Within the process of culling the collection, I was surprised (and delighted) to discover a progressive pattern of transformation, which became the five chapters inside *Sane Response*. These seemed to align closely with Elisabeth Kübler-Ross' five stages of grief.

In the emerging pages of Sane Response, I could see how I had traveled, quite unwittingly, across five stages of "waking up"—*Unknowing, Unwilling, Unwinding, Understanding, Unbound.*

Several close friends, who kindly read my work, encouraged me to share these passages in what is now this book. The idea, they suggested, was that the messages in my poems may meet and support others in their own experiences of loss—loss from divorce, certainly, but perhaps in other manifestations, as well.

With love . . .

Wherever you are on your path of facing loss or disruption, I encourage you to trust the process and trust yourself. Keep going. Keep unraveling what hurts and seeking what heals. You've got this.

More Support for Your Journey

It seems that while every journey from surviving to thriving is unique, collectively, they share commonalities that unify their journeymen. If you are such a journey(wo)man, perhaps you'll access not only poetry, but also our community, to support you in your own arc of healing.

Your Journal Pages...

» You'll find blank pages at the end of each of the five chapters. These are *Your Journal Pages*. These pages invite you to reflect on your own valuable insights—doodle, draw, color; pen a poem; or ponder in prose.

Hear the Poems...

» If your preferred style of "reading" is enhanced through listening, you can hear a recitation of several of the poems online at MollySargent.com/Resources. Or, using your smartphone, you can click on the QR Code, which will transport you to our website. The audio files are under the Resources Tab.

Join Our Community of Support...

» If you'd like further support and community as you travel through the stages of *divorce to discovery*, or of *loss to recovery*, join us at www.MollySargent.com.

We're here for you.

contents

Introduction

"... miracles restore your sanity." ~ A Course in Miracles

xvi   Her Own Sweet Voice

One: Unknowing

Where blind faith prays . . . and plays the fool.

2   Barely Visible
3   A Photograph
4   I Did Not Choose You
8   Little Warning
10   Man-splaining 'Splained
14   He Said / She Said
15   That Awful Woman
16   Tears Again
18   The Room Under the Moon
20   Everyone Has Their Thing
24   Resilient
26   Dead. Gone.
27   Rooted
28   Asleep at the Wheel
30   It Was Years Ago, An Afternoon

32   Your Journal Pages

Two: Unwilling

"Everything I've ever let go of has claw marks all over it."
~ Al-Anon

Someone Else Inhales You	36
Thrust	37
Thinking by the Fire	38
Do Not Deny Me My Sadness	41
First Me. Now Her.	44
Sidewise	46
I'm Angry at My Ugly	48
Lies	50
The Letter I Did Not Send	52
The Warning	54
Dark Night	56
How I Hate You	58
Fear Is a Mole	59
She Waited	60
Cover Me in Soil	62
Your Journal Pages	63

Three: Unwinding

"Go into the darkness, melt away, and emerge."
The caterpillar, she knew what she had to do.

- 68 Why I Came to Maine
- 69 Bird.
- 70 You Come and Go Like That
- 72 The Hug
- 74 My Wise Masseuse
- 76 I Know You Feel Afraid
- 79 Welcome Sorrow
- 80 Free Fall
- 82 The Florist, The Monk and The Mother
- 83 What I Feared
- 84 Absolution
- 86 Over the Reservoir
- 88 Duck For One
- 90 Garden
- 91 Finding My Lover
- 92 *Your Journal Pages*

Four: Understanding

*The future will bring us flowers.
We know because we plant them.*

I am not lost	96
Wee Hours	98
Cricket Song	100
See Him, Fearless	101
Next Time Lover	102
My Ripe Heart	105
A Can of a Soup of Love	106
An Inadequate and Entirely Truthful Letter to My Dear Friend Barbara Who Lives Very Far Away	107
My Dreams Are Blessed by Angels	108
I Want to Love Like . . .	110
Sweet Lover	112
You Can Feel Her	114
Believing Eve	116
It's the Universe You're Talking To	118
Your Journal Pages	*121*

Five: Unbound

"We are all just walking each other home."
~ Ram Dass

126   First Bird
127   How Old Are We When We Are Born?
128   I Came Crawling
131   Wild Iris
132   Hold It Gently
135   Penny
136   In the Language of IS
138   To Become Light

139   Your Journal Pages

Introduction

"By releasing your mind from the imprisonment of your illusions, miracles restore your sanity."

~ A Course in Miracles

Her Own Sweet Voice

There is someone—
	residing inside you or waiting beside you—
	not fully seen, nor heard,
	yet yearning to be.
Please, share with her these poems from me?
	By chance, she may know my voice.
	By circumstance,
	she may find Resonance
	with my words.
	Just as soon, she will encounter

A choice.
My vulnerability will mirror her vulnerability—
	welcome or wearisome,
	comforting or uncomfortable.
Understandably, she may be
	reluctant
	to acknowledge our connection,
	lest she be, like me,
	exposed by these expressions.

No matter. Resonance,
	not exposure,
	is the point of my writing
	(firstly, resonance with myself).
Being visceral, Resonance
	is its own advocate,
	and will not be ignored—
	not by her, just as it would not be
	by me.

No longer complicit with the dark,
    her many hidden parts
    will demand to be brought into the light,
    refusing to continue out of sight—
    only aided, or resisted, in their wish to reunite
    with her.
Resonance—a passive force—
    becomes a choiceless choice.

So remind her (will you, gently?) how Resonance—
    for her, as for anyone,
    in poetry, songs, sex, a walk in the park—
    yields connection.
    Oh, how she craves connection
    (firstly, with herself).

I send love to her
    through, and in, and by these words.
    (I encourage her to write down hers.)
May she find Resonance—and welcome its choice—
    in her own sweet voice.

One: Unknowing

Where blind faith prays . . . and plays the fool.

Barely Visible

I'm having a teary day.
It's part of a teary week.
My guard was down when I asked you
for attention—you,
whom I had assumed
had attention on hold, just for me.

To learn that no such reserve was in waiting,
that no such regard was safeguarded,
well, I tell you,
that was . . .
Well, that was . . .
Something . . .
Something, truly sobering . . .
If I'm honest.

And then tears came up,
like when blood seeps from a paper cut,
the wound barely visible
but the bloodshed, prolific.
So, I did what one does not to sully the couch
nor the moment:
I put pressure on the part that hurt,
bound it tight so it would stop oozing,
and went on with what I'd been doing.

Only, once in a while,
I catch my breath
when the cut hurts
just a bit.

A Photograph

He wanted me.
More than wanted me. He was glad of me.

It's in the photo. Grainy.
On a trip, some place exotic,
carved stone, ancient, gray, and rough.
An arch, perhaps a temple, is in the background.
Indonesia? Malaysia? In the Far East, certainly.

But look. Look at him. His smile is broad. He eyes
the camera, beguilingly,
perhaps aware of his beauty,
perhaps aware of our beauty.
(Did a fellow tourist take this photo?
It's been so long. I can't know.)
His arm, languid, rests around my shoulders. He appears to
　want it there.

And look. Look at me. My head thrown back. I'm
laughing.
(Did some clever quip pass between us?
By the look of us, it seems it.)
No reservations on my face, no fear. No sense
that this is fleeting.

I Did Not Choose You

I did not choose you,
My heart simply knew you—
		immediate and complete,
			your presence resonated with every part of me.

I did not think to be with you;
I simply felt you.
		In one moment, I neither knew you,
		nor knew of you,
		and in the next, you were in my every cell,
inextricably,
		a convergence of two raindrops on a windowpane,
			independently racing along the glass, then
colliding,
instantaneously
		becoming one, ever more unrecoverable
			as two.
Or so I thought.

I did not see you,
so much as perceive you
		in that first instant,
		more sonar and sensing than eyes and vision.
You were simply present to me,
as one feels the presence of another person
entering a room, and
		without needing to look up
		from their writing,
		their reading,
		their crossword,
they know the other is,
		indeed,
		nearby.

I was not awake to the stirring
    that brought you to me,
    that brought me to a space
    beside you.
I imagine falling leaves might be just as oblivious
    to the gentle wind that orchestrates
    their meeting,
mid-air,
    orbiting one another in their descent,
    and landing, tip-to-tip,
    on soft grass.

Once I felt you—familiar, if unexpected—*then*, perhaps,
there came a conscious choice.
Not a balancing of pros and cons; more
    an acceptance,
    like finding money in the pocket of an old coat
      and,
    without recalling how it got there,
    smiling and claiming it.

Once I embraced you,
my arms, outstretched,
could not remember
    not embracing you,
      my every reach wishing
      to catch you in its hold.
My eyes, hungry,
could not see enough of you—
    your silhouette, a reference
    for all silhouettes,

       your face, the pattern
       by which to measure every face.
My ears, relentless,
tuned themselves to the music of you—
       your laughter,
       your word play,
       your footsteps,
       your heartbeat,
dismissing other sounds as white noise,
       undeserving of attention.

I wonder at all that has transpired.
I wonder at
       what I did or didn't;
       what I might have, could have, would have,
if only.

A batter in a dugout—
       post-game, amidst empty stands and
       crushed popcorn containers—
might equally wonder
about the errors that brought on
strikes one, two, three.
Nothing to be done,
       save accept,
       leave the bench, shower, shake it off,
       exit the stadium, enter the night, cap in hand.

It's puzzling, to have loved you so thoroughly,
and to realize
    it was not enough.
A realization, like "there is no Santa Claus."
But more:
    Good guys finish last.
    Hard work does not pay off.
Still more:
    Rivers do not flow to the sea.
    The sun will not rise on tomorrow's horizon.
    Blood, somehow, is not thicker than water.

If I were to bleed,
I would have sworn that your blood would flow
from my veins.
But now, I see—I am bleeding
    without you.

Little Warning

In the quiet light of not-yet-day,
a chipmunk pads across the bluestone
along the crumbling stone wall.
Birds at the feeder chirp,
and a chirp
echoes in return from high
in the pine.
A thousand crevices—between
moss-covered rocks and among
flower beds in full festoon—
hide more chipper voices.
A chorus.

The chipmunk, lollygagging
in quiet consideration
of micro-morsels
below the picnic table,
is unaware of

The Dog.
In an instant,
from peace to beast
leaping the foot of the chaise,
a chase,
a race
for survival, fleeing,
finding

a crevice, disappearing
averting
disaster. Oh . . .

That chipmunk (and I)—
such
a rush
of adrenaline
disrupting
our morning routine!

Settling down again,
I sip my coffee
feeling the dew
of this morning in June,
when

with little warning,
you storm outside, arriving
with a jangle

something angry about your car keys . . .

Man-splaining 'Splained
for men (and women) who might need to know

"So, listen," I'll begin.
"The truth is . . ."
I'll lay that in
early, to settle any doubt
that what I'm about
to say
might be, in any way,
less than settled thinking.

Without blinking,
I'll continue with the floor,
choosing to ignore
the efforts of a brave few,
who
operate under the impression
that we're having a conversation,
and who entertain the idea
that my ideas are open to discussion.

"Here's the thing."
This I'll say, declaratively,
giving it a ring
of being undeniably
true. This, I do
by virtue
of my tone,

simultaneously suggesting that I'm alone
in bringing
considered thinking
to the table.

"Well, yes, I'm uniquely able . . ."
I'll give assurance
in a humble brag of compelling performance,
"to wax philosophic
on this very topic . . ."

This assertion I'll posit
when you implore
to know my source.
"Of course!"
I'll appear to agree,
solicitously,
if you persist in your inquiry,
perhaps begging me to produce my CV.
"Well, now, we can't have you feeling insecure!"
This I'll follow with a snort,
the dismissive sort.

I'll attribute my erudite ability
of knowing more
than most
(again, a necessary humble boast)
as due to my experience,

and hence,
my authority.
I'll then double down on the irrefutability
of my statement,
by inquiring, in the negative,
"Don't you see?"

Any response to this, other than concurrence,
will not serve, mind you, as a deterrent
to my continued opining.
Your sighs I'll just label as jealous whining
and turn to the room
or to those on Zoom
with a knowing glance.
This gives everyone a chance
to shelter themselves in complicit forbearance
of oppositional opinions—
clearly errant—
by under-informed minions,
speaking up, evidently, impulsively.

After this digression
in our discursive session,
I'll resume with my knowing stance
(offering another knowing glance)
to ensure I've been clear,
beholding the gathering, as if from a pulpit,
while contentedly thinking: how fortunate
I am here.

With interlaced fingers to cradle my cranium,
and elbows akimbo,
I'll take up space to the maximum,
and tipping my chair back to teeter on two legs
while side-eyeing the talent (clearly the dregs),
I'll deliver my wisdom with the aura of axiom,
a method I've mastered to combat meeting tedium.

Then,
in a tonal crescendo, I'll end.
"Any questions?" I'll say (shaking my head no),
and quickly follow
with "And so,
I think we can all agree . . ."
(my head, meanwhile, nodding heartily).

After which,
the group's wide-eyed stares
will appear to me
as the well-earned respect
of a fraternity.

He Said / She Said

She said that she said
What she said
Because he said
That instead
They should just . . .

Then, he said
It was her moods
Which made her mad—
Though perhaps it was true—
But wasn't it his moods, too?
It wasn't clear.
So now they're here.

They said
That they said
What they said
To put the past to bed
But all those words, instead,
just made a bigger mess.

There seemed a lot of
Settling scores
Tallying wrongs
Comparing who's wrong more
Because it could only be fair if . . .

Perhaps if
One or both could recall
The moment by the waterfall
The moment they chose to bet-it-all
Then gave the minister a late-night call
And pledged their hearts for all
time.

That Awful Woman
a forgiveness challenge

When she died
I never cried.
My heart had known
too much hurt
at her hands
and by her words.

I'd long since understood
how her sad past
had made her such a poisonous asp.
But while this explanation
provided sense in the sense-making,
it fell short in the excuse-taking.

I had no use on earth
for believing in heaven or hell.
But with her passing, well . . .

Tears Again

Damn. Tears again.
Yeah . . .
They come up when
I suddenly remember when.
Like just back there,

I saw some guy in the grocery line—
    tallish
    with your hair
    standing unaware
    while I tried not to stare.
I put eggs on the belt, quickly wiped an eye,
    and admitted to myself—no,
    I'm not doing fine.

You walked out. Or did I push you?
    Does it really matter when I still miss you?
    I thought this had passed, that my heart made it
      through,
    yet closing my eyes doesn't change the view.
Sometimes, at home,
    I'll pretend I'm not alone.
    I'll sit by the fire,
    with two glasses of wine,
    and talk out loud about old times.
I'll recall how it feels to feel your smile.
    Hard to believe you've been gone a while.
    My memories, forgiven in a bittersweet haze,
    leave me wishing we'd not gone our separate ways.

Sure, it's for the better,
        but it wasn't all bad,
        and that's why, sometimes, I just want what we had—
        so, I drink the whole bottle,
        and don't make it to bed.

You broke us up. Or was it I?
        I try my best to justify
        why we ever said good-bye.
Sure . . .
        It's been years,
        but still . . .
        here come more tears.

The Room Under the Moon

for Kelly M, getting well again

There was no place
That felt safe
When the mother, herself,
Was made pregnant, again and again,
With self-loathing.
She birthed them
One by depraved one
Into the hands of a man—
Always a man
Who pretended to pray—
Who pronounced them dead
Though they defied him
With breath sucked, clandestinely,
Into their forming lungs
Inside rooms where the moon hung
Against an open night sky.

Beneath this blackness
These fledglings tugged
At flattened breasts
Already desiccated
By demand. There was little rest
For mother
For child
For whom each delivery
As with each sunrise

Promised another day
Of oppressive heat
And the only water,
Reservoirs of salty tears.

It was years
Before I found a safe place.
It was years.

Everyone Has Their Thing
thank you, Katie & Gay Hendricks and the #ULP (look it up)

Everyone has their thing,
I suppose,
>the hardship
>the hurt
>the moment (many) of being misunderstood
>cowed
>lonely in a crowd.

Every child starts out,
we can suppose,
trusting,
vulnerable in their trust,
and then—
>by ignorance,
>by willfulness,
>by the pain that begets pain—

the child of trust
comes to know
(in their smallness)
>neglect
>abuse
>confusion
>heartbreak.

It lingers—
the child's
sadness
(which some label as badness)—
hides out
where it's safe.
(Hiding is safe.)

It gets closeted—
the child's
budding singularity
(construed by some as blooming depravity)—
like so many expressions
of who we are
or hope to be—
The parts others can't
or won't
see
The parts not safe
to let free.

Without care,
it grows—
the child's
        sorrows
        disillusionment
        defensiveness
        resentment
        anger
        scorn—
Like mushrooms
        in darkness
        under floorboards
        harmless
        undetected
Until . . .

She had designs on greatness
and love
and accomplishment.

She had a vision
when she was small
for it all
but then
(and she couldn't see why)

Just as she was near
      each destination
      each achievement
      each golden ring of her dreams
      it seems
She'd fail
do something destructive
      (often self-destructive)
      some version of hesitation
      that put the breaks on
      her motivation
      (a wobbly bike
      losing momentum)
She'd fall
and could only explain it all as
"Not me,
obviously.
Logically,
    it's reasons
    one,
    two,
    three."

She couldn't see that
everyone has their thing,
she has her thing—

      a hardship
      a hurt
      a moment (many) of being
      misunderstood
      cowed
      lonely in a crowd.

In time
(and she was blind to this)
her thing outgrew its containment—
      like mushrooms
      in darkness,
      popping floorboards and nails,
      no longer harmless—
a child in pain who
could not grow up
would not grow up
      (though she grew
      bigger,
      bolder,
      older)
waiting
for some grown up
who's actually grown up
to show up
and love her,
      even the hurt parts
      (especially the hurt parts)
      unconditionally.

Yeah, I see.
I've been waiting
for me.

Resilient

I failed my children
In a thousand ways, on a thousand days.
I hurt their hearts
when my heart, first, was hurting.
Their worried eyes
begged me to be other,
to be mother.

At times, I could not.
Could not unfold my brokenness to form
a hollow for their fledgling forms.
I remained as I, too, had arrived, fetal,
my resolve, feeble,
barely sufficient to keep a tenuous hold on a tilting earth.

Ah, but they—resilient,
older than their years of feeling grass beneath
small feet—
stood, grounded, pillars
I leaned on
until I could stand on
my own,
again and again.

I attempted, after each collapse,
to take my place back
at the top of the totem, but saw,
as I needed to—with awe—
the illusion of me as Elder and they as Young
needing molding.

Indeed, it was in beholding,
with admiration and gratitude,
the beatitude
of them—innately strong and wise—
gifts that they, as infants, did devise
to deliver into this world
when their protective postures of the womb fearlessly
   unfurled,
never breathing a word, save
"Forgiven."

Dead. Gone.
#metoo

Few teeth remain in your head,
        Old Man, dying on that bed.
With your days nearly finished,
        your frame seems too diminished
        for the harm you brought
        and the fear you wrought
        and the hell you caught
All for naught
        once the fields of your interment
        clover over
        and the wild fox
        saunters above you
        with no scent of you
        On its way to the nourishing river.

Dead. Gone.

Rooted

The tree root wrapped itself around
the stone, seeking ground, and more ground,
into and through
a razor thin divide,
emerging on the other side,
widening the stone's crevice from inside.
A curious alliance.

Did the tree presume too much
in its progressive binding with the passive rock?
Its roots acted instinctively to grasp
whatever it encountered on its wending path,
anchoring itself by what it clasped.

Did the rock consent
to be conjoined in such a way?
It had been conscripted before, of course,
by a heaving earth and storms,
into positions, indifferently giving perch
to nesting critters.

We might agree the rock's passivity
offered a form of agency.
Conversely, it was the tree
that gave no room for debate,
more entanglement than embrace,
calling out by inches,
"Mine."

Asleep at the Wheel

Wait, what the hell . . . ?
All that time,
asleep at the wheel?
I kinda remember . . . the ride . . .
I kinda realized . . . it's a course to collide . . .

Well, damn . . .
now it's all just too far gone.
Having steered myself so wrong,
Am I getting mine for what I've done—
decisions made
wasted days
when I stayed
when I tried
when I cried?

I shoulda, coulda chosen differently,
not chosen roads that delivered me
unwittingly
here. But admittedly,
back then, it all seemed out of my control.
Of course, now I see the years I stole,
lying to myself. What a fool!

I squandered wealth
and dreams and health.
I have little to show,
it dawned on me slow—

you weren't ever going where I wanted to go.
Well, at least now
I know—

Now
is tomorrow's Then.
Turn around.
Don't do it again.

It Was Years Ago, An Afternoon

It was years ago, an afternoon,
A bright sun bore through dirty windows,
Persistent against my inner gloom,
Reminding me,
Perhaps chiding me, too,
That theres "more and more and more to you."

The prospect of not bearing more weight
      a house
      him
      the business
      kids . . .
So much on my plate,
and I didn't even consider the weight
of myself. Yet of course,
that, too, has mass and density,
increasing the intensity

of the load. I could see it going either way.
My mother had found her way
to leave,
to leave behind
the relentless grind.
Why not I?

It was the dust that caught my eye,
dust that, in its presence,
made the unseeable seen,

a light beam.
Strangely, I could feel
the undulating rays
warm me to the notion
of another moment of another day.
I suppose that you could say
that I'd begun to pray.

"Don't let me leave." But more.
"Don't let me leave before . . ."
Breathless, I chose to breathe.
"Don't let me leave before I've done what I came here to do."
Complete.

It seems every day since,
that same providence
has guided me,
a presence beside me,
not removing dishes, diapers, deadlines, divorce.
Simply pointing out the sun beyond the dirty window,
the yellow moon in the black sky,
the laughable irony
of me
being angry at him for being angry at me.

That is how I learned to pray.
Meeting the moments that make up the day.

Your Journal Pages

*I had my reasons to believe my bliss.
there was that ... and that ... and this ... and this ...*

Your Journal Pages

Two: Unwilling

"Everything I've ever let go of has claw marks all over it."

— Al-Aanon

Someone Else Inhales You

I don't miss you. Not much.
I don't miss how it felt dangerous
To laugh in your presence.

I don't miss you like I used to, now,
Especially not the second-guessing how
I arranged peas on your plate.

I don't miss wondering how to exhale. No,
Nor nervously thinking, once again, I'd failed you
With pulp in the OJ. (Or was it no pulp?)

You shrugged me off, an old robe,
Left pooling on the bedroom floor, and you drove
Away. At first, it hurt, but less each day.

I do miss, perhaps a little, your salty smell,
Inhaled when I held you. Okay, well,
I miss some parts of you. A few. One or two.

Now someone else inhales you.

Thrust
for masculine energy (and onomatopoeic terms)

Thrust your sex at the sun
To be swallowed whole
By burning tendrils, enveloping
First your man's organ, and
Unsatisfied,
Setting fire to your soul.

Be grateful for the ashes that remain
Of what once was you, for
While many exalt the phoenixes—
And you may be, among them, a rarity—
Both cautionary and prescriptive, heed:
They define themselves from burst to burst,
And seldom lose their thirst for thirst.

Thinking by the Fire

Boots rest, unlaced,
cast off on the carpet, both shag and shoes
the muted tones
of which Eileen Fisher would approve.
My back eases its grip on the day,
warmed past the point of being okay
by a fire behind me, which
I'd lit with the flick of a switch
"in the gentrified style,"
I assure myself, "of my former lifestyle."

This is not where I wanted to be—
by a tidy fire,
in tidy suburbia.
This is not how I wanted to live—
hemmed in by salt-of-the-earth people,
our houses showing signs of wear.
I notice, with discomfort, that I care.
The problem, I realize, lies there.

I've questioned myself often since the divorce.
Our splitting was easiest, in that, of course,
it was the healthy choice.
But they don't warn you ("they" who,
to my anxious mind, probably knew
of the coming tumult I'd face).
They don't tell you how divorce creates
paucity . . .

Sheesh. Eye roll. I agree . . .
even my drama queen knows this is hardly poverty . . .
But it's not merely about making
a new life with less money,
       it's the fewer hands to help
       it's rebuilding with half the energy
       it's the surprising silence of certain friends
       it's less contact with his half of the family.

So, I ask of boots and shag,
"How'd we get here?"
Despite the fire, I shiver.
"So, you're ready to go there . . . ?"

When he and I first met, I had my dream.
We shared it, or so it seemed.
All we needed was partnership
and grit.
Perhaps early grooming in piety
blinded me
to the possibility
that we could ever choose to quit.
       Did such naive belief lead me to succeed
       in my work, while ignoring a slow bleed?
       In the distraction of striving,
       did I take for granted our thriving?
       Or did his early capitulation
       to my vision
       finally catch up with him—
       the unbearable strain of a mundane rhythm?

Early in the break up, I came
upon a barely buried shame—
    as I slid down ladder rungs,
    each of which had been hard won,
    feeling queasy
    that they'd give way so easily
    when I'd relied upon them so steadily—
it was a lot to bear,
but I saw it there:
    the folly of my scaling.

I had clambered up, I tell myself, less
to claim victory than to outpace failing.
    I'd come from less,
    and I must confess,
    I was impressed
    to learn how the power of privilege expands
    when even modest riches meet social standing—
No matter if gained by effort, legacy or luck—
    they collude.

"Now, what am I to conclude?"
I ask of elbows leaning on knees,
  wishing for words to appease me.
"Your power is now in the yielding."
  Damn. It's the answer I was expecting;
  just one I've resisted accepting.

I put my boots back on,
  pulling hard at the bootstraps.

Do Not Deny Me My Sadness
for the friend

Friend, do not deny me my sadness.
Yes, bring your understanding—
    and maybe a casserole—
But if it's too much to stay
    beside me in my mourning,
    go away.

Harsh, I know,
    but your gift is fixing,
    and I'm not ready
    to be fixed.
To you, it may appear
    that I'm stuck here
    wed to my bed, my couch, my empty stare
    out the window,
    consuming less food than is good,
    less water than I should.
    (Maybe make some tea?)
But you see,
    I think there's something here
    for me,
    for now,
    if somehow
    I stay, unwavering.
Sadness, I had heard, would be bitter,
    yet it's the sadness I'm savoring.

So, I stay.
And I invite you to stay
    while I dig deep to recover,
    dig deep to discover
    new ways to trust,
    to find kindness, give love,
    from lessons born of
    sorrow,
    to apply tomorrow
    and tomorrow.
To be clear,
    I don't want to be here
    forever. I'll move on—
    probably before all this sadness is gone.
    Eventually, I'll put a patch on the hurt, and
    in time, I'll be fine.
Just not today.

I can't even tell my own heart the timing,
    let alone yours.
    Perhaps this is just how it is
    when one explores
    loss.
So, no,
    I won't be offended if you leave
    while I grieve,
    but I will take offense if you stay,
    and insist that I feel any other way.

Please, check in on me to be sure I'm alive.
    Encourage me, gently, when you arrive
    to change my story
    about things I can't change,
    to find, as they say, the rainbow in the rain.
But also be ready for when my feelings evolve,
    perhaps bringing up anger or fears to resolve.
    For instance, ask me, "What's underneath?"
    if you discover that I'm grinding my teeth.

However you find me, invite me to play.
    Ask that again when I say, "Not today."
    Don't trust my first "I'm not ready yet,"
    but after my second,
you best get
    on your way.
    But promise you'll come back.
    Maybe Thursday?
I wasn't always like this, remember?
    In time—my time—
    I'll be back. I hope, better.
Until then, help me keep the courage
for this unwelcome journey:
    a butterfly, bundled in its cocoon,
    a bud, struggling before its bloom.

First Me. Now Her.
for her (and me)

She's no nonsense (like me), just a bit
(assuming her online persona is legit).
The V at her groin (like mine, I imagine)
a powerful plow:
a bit respite, but also "get shit
done." He's clever to have found us.
First me.
Now her.

He framed photos of our kids for the foyer.
I made scratch from scratch.
We were a match
for a time.
Before we weren't.

She comforts him, I imagine,
like I did,
soothes small scrapes, I suppose
(mostly to his ego).
It's a ritual, habitual,
from a compassionate heart
paired with a pragmatic mind.
Now hers.
Once mine.

Does she get angry? Or shed tears
of frustration?
(I did.
Back then.
Back when.)

He gets fearful
but looks angry
but isn't.
Does she let that lie
just lie there,
like I didn't?

She makes up the "we"
in his stories at parties—
recalling trips to Lisbon
and on safari,
and on his couch watching late night tv.
First it was I.
Now it's she.

I think I'd like her.

Sidewise

I looked at her,
sidewise.
I noticed hollow circles
around her eyes.

A world of worry?
Of sorrow?
Of woe?
I wanted to know
For certain,
So I tried
To peer inside.

Her head seemed to spin
With some swirling mess within—
Stories, perhaps rehashed
In search of wisdom, stashed
Out of sight.
She thought she might—
With each recounting—
Find the reasons why:
    Why they argued.
    Why they said good-bye.

But always the same:
    Plenty of blame
    And none.
        Just a series of deeds done.
They didn't marry
With an intention to fail.
But every effort
Was to no avail—
Tears, bitter.
Discussions, stale.

I looked at her,
sidewise,
in the mirror. She had
my eyes.

I'm Angry at My Ugly
for so many of us girls

My not-ness
has me tied up in knots.
This will surprise no one
who knows one like me.
I'm angry at my ugly.

We grew up learning what beauty is,
what's good.
Was it not universally understood,
well advertised,
and doubly, advised
by parents, partners, pundits, and peers?
They all seemed to make it perfectly clear—

you've simply got
to have what they've got—
    the pretty
    the wealthy
    the skinny
    the healthy
    the famous
    the few.
If that's not you,
well then, you're ugly.

Who first told me this
(no doubt, smugly)?
And who am I—
who was I—
to believe it?

"Just leave it,"
you tell me.
I tell me that, too.
Easy to say.
Harder to do.

Lies
for recovering Catholics and the ilk

There were lies upon lies
I'd heard and heard—
like a golden cage to a resplendent bird,
or a bite in the night from a venomous snake,
or a chain to contain the dog they'd forsake.

The lies were disguised
As songs I should sing,
Reliable music for my suffering,
A chorus trained on my youthful ear,
A constant hymn in the key of Fear.

These lies appeared to me as friends.
I couldn't know their hurtful ends,
Preying upon my innocence.
Smiling wretches, cunning, two-faced.
I never guessed my affections were misplaced.

Who can say
On which day
The shroud of my blindness fell away?
Face to the sun
I beheld the sky
And found my joy there
By and by.

Then truths—sweet truths!—
Arrived as mighty swords
To cut the venom from false words.
Truths sprung the bird,
Unleashed the dog,
Released me, at last, from my complicit fog.

Now truths—my truths!—
I choose, I choose.

The Letter I Did Not Send
for those intrepidly writing for an audience of one

At first, my words came in a trickle
of black ink
penned with precious precision—
      little, prim letters
      inside little, prim squares
      on pretty, grid paper
      of neat, blue lines—
a meticulous letter.

Soon, however,
the trickle began to build, becoming
urgent—
      a surprise of thoughts
      never expressed,
      long repressed,
      about events not explored
      and feelings long ignored,
Until in rapid succession,
      a disorderly torrent
            overtook reason and pen, black ink
                spilling with emphatic strokes, stoking
                an anger larger than the confining lines
                on the limiting page, and I could finally
                feel my outrage, *vividly* . . .

"Wait!" My head chastened me,
      reminding me of a vague moral code—
      "Take the high road."

No!
I (and my pen) would have none of that.
We took the very, very low road. We spoke
      plainly, unevenly, hyperbolically—
I felt grateful for pen and page,
      companions to validate my rage,
      reflecting it back in black and blue,
      a commiseration, making it true,
a dam that broke in me,
      spewing pent-up sentiments, festering resentments,
      floods of profanity, *crashing*
            over confining canyons of polite demeanor,
            breaching boundaries insufficient to contain
            the raucous reservoir of painful memories,
                unleashed, erratic and dramatic—*rush-*
                    ing . . .
until at last . . .

We arrived,
my pen and I,
an inky puddle on paper,
    all the vitriol
    and the sorrow,
    spilled, and seen.

No need to send.

The Warning

We'd been laughing,
He and I,
Easy. He was funny,
Approachable despite his money.
I'd come alone—
It took all my courage
To leave home.
I'd known him from the city,
And from another party or two.
He asked, "How are you?"
The question offered refuge.

She entered with an entrance,
All eyes halting
Upon her statuesque silhouette.
Oh, before I forget:
She's a model.

For a moment
He was extolling me
With a story—charming . . .
Her rapid passage past canapés,
A beeline—alarming . . .

Arriving,
She interlaced her elbow
With his elbow,
Her other hand a fan
On his cummerbund,
Her casual peck to his cheek,
A gesture, measured, sleek.

Before her head turned,
Her eyes turned—
They burned,
Meeting mine
Just above my glass of wine,
A wordless warning:
He's mine.

Dark Night
again, thank you, friend

I'm holding my heart aside,
hands cupped 'round,
blocking the slightest sound
of whispered worries,
or even of rain clouds in a hurry.
Tonight, all winds and whispers strike
as swords might.

Mine is, usually, a heart quite mighty.
But its greatest strength—ah, the irony—
is its vulnerability.
> Alert, it detects a menacing tone.
> Alive, it protects by being alone.
> Angry, it deflects any remedy,
> shaming itself for its propensity
> to trust, unreservedly.

Thank you for understanding.
I'm sure you are wondering
if it's safe to approach me again?
I assure you, I'll let you know when.
Until then,

Best to keep your worries and your wisdom to yourself.
I haven't the fortitude
nor the capacity for gratitude
to welcome the wealth
of your insight.

Tonight
is a dark night
for my heart
and soul.
For now it feels safest
to face it
alone.

How I Hate You
an ode to my projections

How I hate you.
How I hate how I feel being near you.
    You walk away.
    I walk away.
    I'm alone.
      It's another day.
How I hate how I feel being far from you.
How I hate how I feel . . .

How I hate.

That
is what I must heal.

Fear Is a Mole

Fear declares, sincerely,
its insular reality.

Its sights, narrow,
it announces, in truth,
as would a mole
within its burrow:
"It's dark!"
on a sunny day.

True for the mole.
Not true for the lark,
outside, at play.

She Waited

She couldn't get past the threshold, she
later told me—
the big house, the big car, the big social circle
I'd built around me—
though she was keen
to meet.

For a time, I didn't know she existed;
she and all her wisdom.
She persisted.
She looked on, she said,
never very far from me. Often very near.

My mother died,
and when I cried,
she tried then, the dear,
but I was too bereft to hear.
Soon enough, a new wave of responsibility
arose, demanding all my energy.
I lapsed back into the folly of busy,
which masquerades as happy.
Seeing me, once again, preoccupied
by the priorities my life supplied,
she did more of what she'd always done—
she waited.

With hindsight, I see
what I couldn't see then:
I was both blind to my hell
and doubtful of heaven.
But then one day,
the threshold gave way—
vividly, and on public display—
constructed, as it was, on wishful thinking
and wild denial.

For a while,
I sat
staring at the debris of my tumbled illusions,
finally facing the uncomfortable conclusions
       about when, and how, I surrendered my choice;
       about why I compliantly muted my voice.

Surrounded, as I was,
by a sobering silence,
it was then that her voice,
at last, caught my ear—
"Welcome home, dear.
There's nothing to fear."

Cover Me in Soil

Cover me in soil
when my heart has gone to seed—
look for burdened branches
whose fruit
when felled
must bleed.

I and you
and every moon
obscures somewhere the sun.
So, send me back
deliver me back
hands to pungent earth.
Return me there
cover me where
my ribs were formed at birth.
By the woodlands
near the sea
with fragrant darkness
cover me.

Then watch
oh, watch
where Winter's cloak
slips softly as she slumbers
revealing a belly, rounded
and ripening toward summer.

Your Journal Pages

... I understood
love meant taking risks,
 but now tears fall
  on my clenched fists ...

Your Journal Pages

Your Journal Pages

Three: Unwinding

"Go into the darkness, melt away, and emerge."
The caterpillar, she knew what she had to do.

Why I Came to Maine
for Sarah, Connie and Dianadonn

Tufted reeds belie the shadow
Where a footpath snakes the golden meadow.
Footfall, footfall, sure and slow,
Drum patient progress to the shores below.

Inhale, exhale, in gentle flow,
My breath joins waves lapping to and fro
Over broken shells that shimmer like snow
And rustle in the swale with quiet echo.

Brooding clouds, misty and low,
Hug the harbor with its boats in a row.
A single sail, released in a billow,
Cups September's chill in its leeward hollow.

My wistful eyes give steady follow,
Past the horizon toward a trust of tomorrow.
In Maine, there's a place where I like to go
To still my heart, and perhaps to borrow
From a peace that finds hope within my sorrow.

Bird,
for Diana and Vermont

Bird,
You are so very, terribly red,
chest puffed into the rising sun.
Your magnificence—not pride,
but nor do you hide—
is simply shared
from your perch up there in the tall pine.

Such is my observance of you
from my own perch. Mine
sits past the green trees
in the brown house
where I sip tea.

I'm so grateful for your bold display.
I think I'll wear red today.

You Come and Go Like That

for those who loved Tommy, #guncontrol

I'm reaching back,
fishing for grocery totes from the rear seat,
a mechanical act.
Suddenly,

I'm thinking back—
You are next to me.
"I'll get the bags and meet you inside," you say.
I stay
in the dream, my twisted frame, frozen
lest you disappear.
The choice causes me pain.
It eases it, too.

Back then. A moment. You—
back when you looked at me,
laughing, loving.
Your eyes, I remember, were soft.
Your hand on my arm, gentle.
Your smile, wide,
all teeth and crinkled nose.

Now, I sit with you.
There are no words.
You are just as I need you to be—
adoring, beside me.

Blink. A tear upon my cheek,
wet, brings me back to the steering wheel.
My eyes squint against a glint
of reflected sunlight through dirty glass
from a car trying cautiously to pass
pedestrians caught up in conversation.

Slowly, I become aware,
outside the open window, there,
wafting lilacs ask for appreciation.
I resent the honking horn,
the lilacs, and the sun.
They're outside this car
where, for a moment, you are.

Still reaching back,
with my mind twisting like my form,
I fish again for the thread
Of you. Instead,

the bags.
I close my fingers around them.
Pull them to my chest.
Today, it seems, must be lived
while you come and go like that.

The Hug
for Heidi & her Larry

Softly,
I wrap you to me,
as if
(if only)
to absorb, a bit,
your pain,
a weight too great
for just one to contain.

A sea.
Your unfocused eyes suggest
its depth
and turbulence,
encroaching with slow patience
upon your last scrap of forbearance.

Beyond
our ring of arms,
its volume defies
my wish to provide
relief—
albeit brief—
a mere teaspoon extracted
from its fathoms.

From your dark fathoms.
Even still, my meager embrace,
perhaps guided by grace,
takes liberty to be expressed—
    being a language wordless
    and spoken since all time;
    spoken before this terrible time.

"That terrible time"
we will call it
some day
far away
from here—

From the rambling house you inhabit,
each room comfortless,
nonetheless,
willing us
to stay—
   you being obliged to obey,
   I will it, too,
   becoming still in it
   with you—

Until
the rabbi is through,
and the headstone is in the rear view,
and the hollow
of my insufficient hug
carries away
what it can
of this terrible time of you.

My Wise Masseuse
for Tali and all the healers

Her words came back to me
in the dark closet where I took refuge
from people
who couldn't understand
how the air out there was stifling, and
how tears can be felt,
though not seen.
My trusted masseuse had kneaded with words
I didn't know I needed;
and besides, until now,
I wouldn't have believed it.

"Turn your eyes to the night sky. Peer there
at sparks of light
and arcs of light,
skittering.

I've seen them through a camera lens,"
she whispered this bit of Zen,
as though letting me in
on a secret.
"Give these bright orbs your problems
to be lifted and shifted,
stirred and returned to you
different,
often, full of wisdom.
Then hold what's healed," she told me.

In the dark closet, far from her healing hands
(and with little to lose,
if this touch
of fairy dust
didn't prove to be true),
      my shoulders relaxed and
      my jaw unclenched and
      my heart felt light and
      my chest felt warm and
      my limbs felt shivers
      run down them.
I let her angels in.

I Know You Feel Afraid
another anniversary

Friend, I know you feel afraid.
But, you and I have heard it said:
    fear requires our complicity
    before it can define our reality;
    only our indulgence gives
    credence to its story
    and power to its power.
Instead,

Breathe.
Breathe into the quiet place in you,
    beyond the noise that pretends
    to know *for* you.
Knowing *for* you
    is *your* work to do.

Be still.
In your stillness, be patient.
Sometimes, the quiet place waits
    to speak, first gauging
    your sincerity,
    before navigating
past the well-honed resistance
    of your mind and habits.

Listen.
In your listening, attune your ear.
    The quiet place articulates
    its wisdom as resonance.
As you learn to better hear,
    its wisdom will become
    more and more clear.

Trust.
Once you receive the gifts
    your quiet place bestows,
    trust that you're the only one
    who needs to know.
Later, you might share
    what was shared with you
    but only with others who trust
    as you do.
Take care to choose those others wisely;
    don't invite their doubt
    about what you found out.
Having listened with your heart,
    ask others (the few) to simply start
    to wonder *with* you
    at the meaning of the messages
    from your quiet voice in your quiet place.

Be grateful.
What the quiet place reveals to you,
    it does so for your sake, not its own.
The quiet place has no ego
    tied to your belief;
    its gifts flow,
    regardless of who chooses to receive.

Converse in the quiet place,
if you are inclined.
    When you talk back, you'll find
    its answers reside inside—

    in words and images that come to your mind,
    in vibrations that travel along your spine.
Ask it to repeat itself so you feel sure—
wait 'til you feel
   warmth in your belly
   and tingling on your skin.
Peace is the surest sign you're letting its wisdom in.

Leave the quiet place.
Follow its counsel. Then
   go back again
   for more and more,
until the quiet voice
in the quiet place
   is the only voice you need;
   the only voice you heed.

Welcome Sorrow

Sorrow, I hear,
is visiting you, dear
friend.
For your sake, please
let him in.

His knock is loud
and insistent,
and he will wait,
persistent,
at your door.

You don't need to allow him
a lengthy stay.
I've heard from others
who cooked for him and lay
his bed with downy comforters—

It's the sincerity of your welcome
in which he finds his satisfaction
and soon enough departs,
leaving behind a potpourri
that is not unpleasant.

Free Fall

We do not control what is beyond ours to control.
Yet we wish to.
      Our frustration crescendos
      as we play a fruitless game
      of "what if . . ." and "how should . . ."
I have begun to believe
      that learning to be
      in this swirl,
      while remaining at peace,
      is our very mission in this world.

"Feel it," recommend wind
      and moisture on skin,
      minute to minute,
Making it
a timeless call
      for us all
      to come, quite literally, to our senses.

Alas, visceral attunement has no use for pretenses.
Such alternatives to feeling
are appealing—
      the thinking,
      the doing—
      these feel reassuring,
      yet their artifice—seductive—
      renders experience reductive.

It takes (by my loose calculations) a lifetime (or two)
      of being battered and battling
      before allowing the reality
      of our unthinkable vulnerability
      to sink in.

Once we do, the letting go becomes
    possible,
    responsible,
    inevitable.
A free-fall begins.

Then
having spent endless energies outpacing
such a fate,
our novice natures face
    the groundless, rushing sensation
    of losing control—
and oh, how we wail
    in terror, while flailing,
    frantically clawing
    at traction-less air,
until,
sensing the futility of woe,
    we choose, at last, abandonment of reason, and
        discover
    that our ancient souls

Wake up—
    sprouting wings of courage to meet the column
        of rushing wind,
    not breaking our fall; rather guiding our descent,
        and
guttural,
we exhale with long-held breath, and remember

how to fly.

The Florist, The Monk and The Mother
For Marc

The florist,
The monk, and
No less, the mother,
Give birth to arrangements, mandalas, children
Beautiful, precious, impermanent.

Come, now.
Celebrate both the bud and the bloom
That adorn the bride and the groom.
Appreciate, too, the saffron guard
Attentive to their sand art.
Join the family, besotted,
Around the bassinet.

It passes soon.
Petals fall gently from a waist
coat, cast off in haste
by the groom.
Colors collide, at the level of grains,
under the bristles of a monk's broom.
And mother, beholding her child's gray hair,
smiles into her own demise,
satisfied.

What I Feared

Knock. Knock.
The door was locked.
I had taken pains
to barricade
against what I feared—still,
they came.

I made them wait,
my being in a nervous state.
I took my time to get presentably dressed,
so they wouldn't guess
at my distress
for having messed up the life plan.

I stopped to straighten the room—a delay,
since it appeared
they were here
to make me pay.
I'm not a fan of castigation.
Yet here I was: guilty by habituation.

Eventually, though,
as I fluffed another pillow,
I realized they weren't likely to go,
so, I opened the door
and allowed the flow-in
of the I-Don't-Know-What's-Coming.

And well, well, well,
you'll never guess?!
Indeed, hard truths flowed in, yes,
but each also rendered me
kindly blessed.

Absolution
for Annie and Cape May Point

Wrap 'round me, Sea,
And leave me
Bathed, though I be broken—
By you, little is said,
Yet much is spoken.

It's not your job to forgive,
I know,
Yet your breaking waves
Nudge my heart to live
With their pounding, sure and slow.

For though fair or foul, your froth,
I trust you do not judge,
And rightly, your moods
I don't begrudge,
Since it is I who begs
at your churning edge.

Resolute,
I stand before
You, with pain laid bare
Upon this shore
Begging baptism.
Pray,
Match my salty tears
To your advancing spray,
And on your reversing course,

Bear away
The weight of my remorse.
And if you will, please confide
In me. For before this tide,
O'er a million years
was your wisdom wide.

Sea,
She captured me
In her majestic curl.
I, crestfallen,
Knelt between sand and swirl.
And there, by her nature, buoyant,
Sea lifted my burden,
And invited joy in.

Over the Reservoir
on the late bus from high school

I remember
an occasion mundane—
a time
hard to explain,
yet it left me
with a feeling sublime,
a moment—strange as such—
it hinted at an angel's touch.

As I recall,
the sun was sinking, colorfully,
and I (a much younger me),
on a school bus, was wanting to see
the colors shift, kaleidoscopically,
as we sped along a long, long bridge
spanning a reservoir.

I remember,
then,
the moment when
the creaky bus, inexplicably
slowed to a stop, jerkily,
above the reservoir.

I recall, too,
being ecstatic—
and a bit cracked up—
that a line of traffic
had suddenly backed up.
The bus driver perplexed,
the older kids vexed,

out loud fuming—
would we soon be resuming
our way
across the reservoir?

Even now, I can see
that sun sinking low
across the water, and me
by a window
enjoying the chance
to watch it go
in a blaze of nonchalance
over the reservoir.

I cherish the memory—
thinking "this is just for me"—
as the road cleared
miraculously
and the bus lurched
back into Drive
toward home
on the opposite side
of the reservoir.

I seem to recall,
as I looked over my shoulder,
the sky was alive
with a peach-and-pink smolder
reflected
as fire
in the glass
of the reservoir.

Duck For One

The mailbox door dangles,
Circulars stuffed to overflowing
Mixed with mail I ought to read
Right away.
But probably won't.

A birthday card (oh three!).
How lovely (and old fashioned).
Pink, blue, glitter covered.
These envelopes get sorted out of the stack.
Otherwise, bills mostly.
I leave those on the countertop
Conveniently
Within reach to bookmark
The duck recipe
For one
I'd like to try.

Soy first, or shaved ginger?
Sticky cookbook pages
Cling to a folded reminder
that I'm late on the car payment.
Very late.
I add it to the pile of envelopes
Giving perch to the butter dish.

Later that evening,
I drag the recycling to the curb.
A letter escapes from the bin,
Tossed in error?
An insurance copay,

Stating "payment due upon receipt"
That I hope the credit card can handle.
Back in the kitchen,
An opened bank statement
Just under the hot mitts
Tells me the funds are there,
But that was from last month, so
Maybe.

Remember the big house?
We paid every bill on time.
You cut the lawn
And wound the grandfather clock
Precisely.
And I cooked for four
Rather nicely.

Lately
In my small space
The weeds grow tall
The dishes linger
The mail gets stacked
Unattended.

But at least today
The duck turned out okay.

Garden

for Karen & her Jerry in Rowayton

The garden where our roses grew—
The ones we pretended were just for me and you?—
The old gardener came and pruned a few
And cut some for his cottage, too.
I came down here for the pretty view.

Can you see how much I'm missing you?
You went sooner than you were expected to.
Of course, I refused to believe it true
That when you'd leave, you'd leave me, too.
We still had plans of things to do.

How many seasons have we been through
Since we laughed together in this morning dew?
It could be one or twenty-two—
I only keep time as *before* or *after* you.

Velvet petals pad my path,
With every footfall, a fragrant waft
Conjures memories of how we walked among
The blooming hedges before you were gone.

I will continue—I think I must—
To greet the morning and the dusk
Within this garden where the view
Includes a world where there's always you.

Finding My Lover
for the Type A

What if?
To hear my lover, I must learn all the languages of the world,
   in that way to know his words as they are calling me?
What if?
To find my lover, I must live everywhere at once and keep
   my many doors ajar,
   in that way to see him and greet him when he's not far?
And what if?
To feel my lover, I must embrace every person—man,
   woman, child—
   to connect our hearts, chest to beating chest?

How will I know you, lover?
How will you know me?
How will I find you, lover?
I beg you, find me.

"Shhhh . . ." whispered the wind.
"Rest," suggested the stream.
"Dream," instructed the clouds.
A dappled light
offered its advice
while stroking the green grass
where I found repose.
"Wait, a bit, just so."

It was while I slept that my lover came to me
with only my soul awake to sense his gentle approach.

Your Journal Pages

*. . . the hard truth is: there was always this—
        quickened heartbeats and heartbreaks, mixed . . .*

Your Journal Pages

Four: Understanding

The future will bring us flowers.
We know because we plant them.

—Anonymous

I am not lost

I was my own plus one for my own party.
My guests were lovely—
    "I brought wine."
    "Cute pillows! Where'd you get 'em?"
    "How are you? No, *reeeally*."
We had a fine time,
    then as quickly as the dishes were cleared,
    the guests, too, were cleared
    from my mind,

Except you.
With the dishes done,
    I topped off my wine,
    settled on the sofa,
    pet the dog
    while streaming mindless TV,
    and falling asleep
where I dreamed of you . . .

You arrived with the others "to balance the seating."
And with you entered a new calibration
    of my standing place. Strange,
    when I moved,
    I moved toward you or away,
    not quite the center,
    but the sightline,
a clear measure
    of "where am I?"
    that let me know,
"I am not lost."

You left for the last time
much the way you arrived for the first—
    easy in the impulse.
    Did you know you departed with my compass
    in your pocket?
    No mind. With time,
I am not lost.

Wee Hours

The wee hours
bring their blackness,
and I—in lazy lotus,
blanket-wrapped,
Tibetan gong tapped—
breathe out day's "rush!"
breathe in night's "hush..."
sightless eyes on
a lightless horizon.

"Where to?"
A question I ask night's guides—
Journeymen
cloaked in dark robes,
alert with seers' eyes.
"Follow."
I attempt to abide.

In the stillness outside
of my insides,
faint noises
become amplified—
Night owl? Hooved deer?
Shadow sounds,
which the hollow night compounds—
worrying my ear.
"What's that I hear?"

"It's of no matter,"
my guides soothe the chatter
and I return me
to the inner journey.
"Where to?"
I ask again,
and wait for the lead
of the Journeymen.
Again to the meditation,
to the desire for relation,
to the quest for inner elation,
going deeper into silence.

In the wee hours
there is no "should."
Trusting heightened senses,
I feel my way forward.
Soon enough
heat radiates
across core and limbs.
A vision emerges, in which rippled vastness
gives comforting form to endless blackness.
There, with buzzing thoughts sedated,
with impulsive actions abated,
and resonance elevated,
my heart rediscovers how to be elated.

By this practice,
I've come to know,
in the black, wee hours,
I'm not alone.

Cricket Song
For Avan & Michael

Once in a while,
I have this dream:

a lover's heart thrums a lullaby
to my resting frame, and I
sink
without resistance to gravity—emotional and actual—
feeling secure
in the armor of his watch
        Where no touch but his
        disturbs me
        No eyes but his
        observe me
        No scent but his
        occurs to me
I, childlike,
yet fully grown
Resting,
slowly silencing
the deafening
sound of my own vigilance,
Allowing
space for cricket songs—just outside—
to rise,

an anthem to match my peace.

See Him, Fearless

for Andrea in Rowayton

See him, fearless, dip his wing?
How are we just so?
Sensing currents with sightless ease,
Knowing, though we cannot know.

By heron's flight, inspired,
Imagining there my Joy,
I call myself to a Courage
My lesser Will might ignore—

Take the road that calls you.
Trust the voice only you can hear.
Distinguish for yourself what are Wisdom's words
From those that are spoken by Fear.

Choose the Bliss within you,
The calling card of Love,
A story unfolding, truly,
Toward purposes you know not of.

Next Time Lover
for Camden & Taylor

Next Time Lover,
I will tell you that you are beautiful.
And just as true,
I will tell you
how, in your presence,
I feel my beautiful, too.
I will see your gaze
as a lens I borrow—
beholding myself anew
through the eyes of you.

I will tell you how, drawing close to you,
my heart
draws down your fire,
one candle igniting another
emitting twice the light.
And as when a fledgling flame flickers
in the hollow of cupped hands,
my body, too, tingles
with anticipation of heat, yet peace,
in your arms.

Next time,
I will fold myself into you and invite you
to fold yourself into me—
    like a baker's batter
    folded into itself
    over and over
    in a single, stainless steel bowl—yet
yielding two cakes.

When we are away, one from the other,
I will recall you,
not as a yolk nor as a crutch,
neither a shadow nor any such. It's just
I will understand how
a bit of you stays with me,
intricately,
woven like a silver thread
traversing the warmth of a shawl,
gentle, around my shoulders.

I will remind myself, sooner, lover,
that my heart is my responsibility
and your heart is yours, only
I have the privilege
simply
to tend to you and your heart, tenderly,
for a short time.

Next time,
I will know to bring
the wholeness of me
to be
with the wholeness of you,
aware that I must not
come to you
bent on being broken and expect you
to fix me.

I might invite you to share your wisdom,
so that I may better see—and be—myself,
but I will not collapse
and hand away, expectantly,
the source of my joy
my peace
my well-being.
Such trust was charming
but childlike, there
where I once ceased to own
my own creation.

Next Time Lover,
I might ask you
"How do you like to live?" and
I will tell you
"Here's how I like to live!" and
we will answer, again and again,
every morning, knowing
our answers are always forming
from time
to time
eternal.

My Ripe Heart

I offer my heart, lover. Ripe, she's
Shiny as an apple, still wet with morning dew.
Peeled like a banana, her defenses removed,
revealing vulnerable pulp.
Spread open as an orange, fragrant,
her sections, sweet.
She's ready to be consumed,

plump

succulent

savory

and messy.

A Can of a Soup of Love

breathless at MOMA (with my beautiful kids)

I'm full

like a can

of a soup

of love

it's what I'm made of

filled

to the fill line

above even

the spill line

I'm full

to abundant

(redundant)

I live

to love

to know only of

this feeling

An Inadequate and Entirely Truthful Letter to My Dear Friend Barbara Who Lives Very Far Away

for friends who bring us through

I miss you.

Life is happening over here.

No single emotion ("fine," "great," "tiring," "thrilling," "confusing," "heart-warming") will do.

I'm sending you love from all these peaks and valleys.

I trust you're getting my love, because—

even though I'm very far away

and even when I'm having a too-busy day—

my higher being

knows your higher being

since all eternity, and thank heaven,

since all eternity, has sent

love from me to you, often.

Even now.

xo

My Dreams Are Blessed by Angels

Any more
I move
methodically.
It's odd
for me.
I used to be
fast. Now I'm slow . . .
Ya know?

It's not a hip,
nor a sudden slip
I worry about. No,
though
they may be sufficient cause
to pause.

It's a commitment
these days
in my ways
to lift away
the distracting haze
of a busyness
that once garnered praise
from those whose instruction
promotes constant production.

Youthful me
was eager to please.
Perhaps my age
makes me more sage,
for—no more in deference
to others' behests—
my current quest
bids me invest
more time in rest,
wherein my dreams are blessed
by angels.

I know for some
such suspect wisdom
may appear falsely winsome,
yet truer, never,
my thoughts so clever,
and my bounty, too!

My joy is true.

I Want to Love Like . . .
for Honor & Cedrick

"I love."
It was a wind that gently whispered that.
It seemed a simple fact,
no agenda in its caress.
I want to love like that.

I want to love like a footprint loves:
by becoming and being
and testifying by its impression
that in this place, briefly,
such was so.

I want to love like a lighthouse loves:
by shining a light unwavering,
not dimmed by storms. Guiding—
without reciprocity—
anonymous sailors at sea.

I have seen what often passes for love,
but is not:
      forceful and imposing,
      asserting a stealth adamancy,
      assuming another's self-agency,
      assigning fate without diplomacy,
      aided by naive dependency.
This is not the love for me.

I want to love like a firefly loves—by glowing—
and like a flower loves—by growing—
inviting—
with fragile wings that fan
and velvet buds that unfurl—
      the child's unrivaled smile,
      the gardener's tender tear.

I want to love. And you draw ever near.

Sweet Lover

for the dogma-burdened

At last, a safe space
at last, a soft place
a chance to embrace
and to be embraced
with you, sweet lover.

Distant, the race—
        the games I once aced
        as if to outpace
        some guilt with my haste—
all before you, sweet lover.

It was years I misplaced
in which love and disgrace
wore the same face—
        so preached the chaste
        who lived shame-faced
        for whom touch was debased
        who lived to lambaste
        and taught me to place
        my trust in a condemning Other.

With each kiss you place
upon my upturned face,
those years are erased,
no longer a trace
of feeling displaced—
        forgotten, my disgrace,
        like Eve's wanton taste;
        gone each gaze, face-to-face,
        of another and another.

With our ample grace
and our limbs interlaced,
we set our own pace
our moves gently spaced—
shedding caution for passion
consuming love without ration—
we come together, sweet lover.

In your loving gaze
I learn to love in new ways—
trusting
sweet love.

You Can Feel Her

You can feel her, if you're attentive,
the woman, constrained.
For the sake of peace, she's self-contained.
Her entrance is as an afterthought
at the door to the party—
the sack he snatched up
from the passenger seat
as he exited the car. He
was late.

She's eight steps back,
eyes downcast,
a furtive look
when she does look
up, and then, her lips are the thin line
of an efforted smile,
while her eyes attempt to disguise
their uneasy quest for protection
from detection.

You can feel her,
more so since you've known her
from the inside out.
And so your eyes hang longer,
carefully soft, on her

and into her hesitant glance,
when she risks that fleeting chance
      to see you seeing her,
      to see you being okay
      with the way
she's created a fragile balance.

With luck, she'll feel your assurance
that her time will come—
it takes longer for some—
just as your own time came
and now

you are standing there
near her,
your happiness
so close
she could almost . . .

Believing Eve

The scene: Eve under the canopy
of a fragrant apple tree.

Act one: Branches—straining with an abundant crop—
hardly took notice, as errant bushels dropped,
which greedy bees consumed,
freely. All this,
just inches
from where all damnation loomed.

The fruit, it goes, was forever forbidden
(though, clearly, its attractions were poorly hidden).
Given, it's said, Eve's propensity
for unsupervised femininity,
and claiming it best for our maiden,
it was decided
she'd live as a stay-in.

Act two: But sensual she,
hearing the happy, buzzing bee
(and her captor's silence to her every plea)
    took thorough stock,
    broke the confining lock,
    scattered bees and a nearby flock,
    shook the tree,
    took a knee,
    and finally
    ate one, two, three.

Narrator: What are we to believe
of the stories about this early Eve?
Did an impulsive she take reckless leave
    to smell the fermenting fruit that drips,
    to lick the saliva on her lips,
    to follow the pulsing of her hips
    and Nature's whispers of sweet ecstasy?
Was she poorly guided?
Must she be ever-chided?
And must her nakedness be hided
    for all eternity?

What if she had reported, first—
    not he?
What a different tale might there be:
    of courage and curiosity?
    of embracing the abandon of a bee?
    of accepting responsibility?

Epilogue: The tale I sooner do believe:
    Eve chose for herself,
    and Adam got peeved.

It's the Universe You're Talking To
for me

I sat down one day to meditate.
The session's focus was to get a date.
Lest you think me vapid or vain,
let me explain.
My yoga mat and I
had spent the previous day reflecting on world peace,
so the next day, I
gave myself permission
in my spiritual transmission
to engage angelic wisdom
in pursuit of a loving companion.

He'll be funny and clever,
but caustic, never.
He'll abide integrity on topics that matter,
    be truthful but kind, and disinclined to flatter,
    celebrate imperfection,
    be given to inner reflection,
    mindful of his vocal inflection,
    know grammar well, yet be slow with correction,
    and aware of habits like victimhood and projection.
(He'll keep these in mind,
but won't mind them in me.)

More than forgive, he'll fan the flames of flaws,
seeing problems as cause
to become curious with introspection,
going inward for direction.

I like accomplishment in men.
It makes it easier then
for me
to be
extraordinary
as I intend,
so he'll have done
a thing or two,
and won
at least a few.

He would be, for efficacy,
a bit like my family—
like my brothers (I have four),
like them, and more.

Perhaps, he'll be like Jim Carrey,
I proposed
with eyes closed
to the candle.
Someone off kilter but not so much that it's hard to handle.

A voice began to chuckle inside.
"It's the Universe you're talking to."
One eye opened, wide
aware,
then and there,

that the limits of imagination were my own.
I quickly dropped back in the zone,
closing my eyes
(all three),
my prayer revised:
not someone LIKE Jim Carrey,
I said,
THE Jim Carrey, instead.

I sent Jim a message on the astral plane
(that might be hard to explain)
so if you see him, let him know it's me?
I'll set out a pot of fragrant tea,
or if he prefers, a well-aged whiskey.

Your Journal Pages

*... just as true, there's nothing remiss—
nothing wrong
it all belongs ...
even this.*

It's all a gift ...

Your Journal Pages

Your Journal Pages

Five: Unbound

"We are all just walking each other home."

~ Ram Dass

First Bird
for Anne and the sunrise view from dad's house

First bird,

the first heard,

piercing dawn

with shrill song

trilling, trilling

The first one willing—

        as horizon stirs beneath her pale coverlet—

waking the indifferent

for gathering—they, together,

all aflutter,

fussing their feathers,

balanced on a wire,

an entire choir,

a ruckus,

cacophonous.

Daybreak.

How Old Are We When We Are Born?

How old are we when we are born?
Does ancient wisdom
follow us
through the birth canal,
      gasping awake with us
      at the sudden grip
      of strange hands and cold air?

Early evidence would tell us, *No.*
Having forcefully arrived,
each of us appears to begin—
      at the intersection
      where nature and nurture
      meet innocence and ignorance—
      ill-equipped and alone.

But later life, I'm beginning to see,
tells us differently.
With time,
      our nature hints at a smuggler's stash
      of knowing,
      as if our blood-soaked forms emerge,
      cloaking
      a gift from our older, wiser selves.

I Came Crawling

I came crawling
to the calling
of my life,
the calling beyond my strife.
Crawling, because
it took great catastrophe
(well, catastrophe is dramatic,
but definitely it took panic)
to wrest
my attachments from me.
A great mess
and yet, a blessing.

At any time, did I agree
to go through
the ugly upheaval
that would reveal
my facade to me?
Even so, did I ever doubt
that anything but a gobsmacking rout
would be needed to deliver me out
of caring about
how things appear,
of holding up a pleasing veneer?

Whether I did or didn't,
I must admit,
it's a luxury
to watch the old fears fall away.
(Okay, the upending occasion
did not take them all away,
and admittedly it swapped out a few,
equally questionable, though new.)

But here's the point:
      when so much got out of whack,
      I tried to claw it back.
      I wanted stability
        more than liberty
        (the latter, a fearsome responsibility).
Previously, I couldn't see
      the toxicity
      mixed in with the status quo.
(It's the devil ya know.
Ya know?)

Perhaps it was some prayer
I breathed somewhere
(in a dream
it would seem,
for who would ask for such remedy
if they knew it
entailed such ruin?)

In hindsight,
I'd invite
it all, again—
going from a state of holding it all in,
and getting to a state of being all in—
declaring, firstly,
fuck it all, then, rapidly,
    accept it all,
        respect it all,
            bless it all,
                let it all go

and go about your business of
    dispensing love
        and making a difference.

Wild Iris

for Kelly J, equal parts iris and wild

An iris grew

Wild, in a field,

Her purple petals, vibrant

Swaying atop a strong, yet flexible stem,

Her scent sufficiently sweet

For sharing with bees and caring for birds,

Beyond whom no one, no body, no person

Witnessed her.

In time, she—the iris—died,

Each petal, slowly

Loosening its hold,

Descending

With quiet dignity

To the soft grass below

Until she was, no more.

By her measure, what is joy?

Perhaps, not from eyes beholding you;

rather from life unfolding as you?

Hold It Gently

Hold it gently
this life—
joy and sorrow
alike.
Do not believe
that the breadth and distance
of what you see
(what we call reality)
is the totality.
So much resides
beyond our scope of
sight and sound, and
besides

What is tangible is temporal.
Every sense and sentiment is passing.
So, If you're asking
of fixed points
outside yourself
        east / west
        north / south
        up / down
to deliver you to yourself,
these will only begin to begin—
as stars will not hand to the sailor the land,
rather their luminescence hints at its direction.

Instead, we must look for guidance
in an ironic reliance
on change, whose defiance
toward stagnation
will be our salvation,
shedding, too, our commitment
to being right or wrong, or
to understanding it all.
That was never the call.

Indeed, we must go within
to feel
the ballast and balance
in the very motion
that sickens us.
But we, truculent,
are reluctant
to discard the seductive
illusions of steadfastness,
instead,
grasping at its straws of empty promises.

Imagine, then, this:
that the boundaries of body
define only the beginnings
of our understanding

of home.
Within (and beyond) the body
exists the bounty
of every ever.
For before this unknowing,
there existed the Known,
who did not call the body
"home."

Our primary job is remembering—
the calm, the peace, the joy—
all gifts to employ
in our earthly expressions of creation,
discarding the fallacies of damnation,
a mere fear-monger's invitation.

Rest, then, in this:
What's outward lies,
while inward lies the only certainty
that supports you
being here—
and going home.

Love it all,
Beloved.
Hold it all
gently.

Penny
for Lisa & Letty

Heads up penny
Stay where you lay.
I'm already having a pretty good day.
Maybe the mister
Just ten steps behind
Will need what is given
With such a sweet find.

In the Language of IS
for Claire & other ponderers of the ineffable

Before I thought,
I saw.
On a morning walk, I didn't talk
even to myself.
I simply beheld and felt.
A wordless wondering.

Taking to my mode
of poetry and prose,
      I sit here, now,
      and wonder aloud,
      but this time I allow
      intrusions from my pen.

Thus I reprise
my journey of eyes,
recalling fields and skies—
      a vast gateway, simultaneously,
      inviting me into
      and beyond,
      my being.

Entering internal hollows
without the benefit of light,
I see
      radiating heat
      building in the space
      where my ribs meet,
      and moving along my spine and seat,
      down my legs, across my feet.

Returning to where my chest lifts and falls,
and counting its rhythms
from pause to pause,
I see
        my breath as it flows, filling
        my lungs, caressing
        my throat, rising and resting
        at the inflection
        of my widow's peak.

With the guidance of an aura's light,
I, sightless, see
        an eye,
        and I see the eye see me,
        perhaps, each of us
        seeking to know
what IS and who IS
        (in) the language of boundless resonance.

To Become Light

"What is to give light must endure burning." ~ Viktor Frankl

Burn. Become
as a bonfire becomes embers
and ashes.
Preserve nothing of your construct
which might lend itself, otherwise, as light waves
undulating with urgency in search of the Edges of the
   Universe.

We will not find such a Boundary, which does not exist.
Yet out and out and out we are compelled to go,
away from every fallacy of knowing
toward nothing known
there, simply,

forgiving

our many forms their constraints

and willing ourselves

to become light.

Your Journal Pages

. . . and facing forward, I don't resist.
Boldly, I go
to claim my wish . . .

Your Journal Pages

Your Journal Pages

epilogue

Why I Wrote *Sane Response*

When illness shuttered the world, it also temporarily shuttered my 20 year old business. In response, I decided to take to my couch and to write my "lucrative business book." But each time I sat down to "get down to business," my mind, time and pen had other ideas.

Over the course of many months, when my writer's block showed up at my business book keyboard, I indulged in a relaxing and entertaining habit of harvesting my old poems from a trove of decades-old, tattered journals. In due course, this habit of "taking a break by resurrecting my old poetry" resulted in a robust, semi-autobiographical compilation of rhymes and prose. The words and verses—rough and ill-composed in their original forms—were as letters to myself from the many stages of my struggles as a younger woman making her way, awkwardly, through work, love, and life.

As the canon of my writing emerged, I began to see, at the age of 59, what my younger self had been experiencing. I wondered if I might be in a better position—emotionally, spiritually, logistically, financially, intellectually—to mentor my younger self. Might I recast her experiences in the light of my older, more developed perspective, providing context, insight and even practical tools, which she didn't have back in her day, but which I came to possess along our shared path?

Conversely, and fortuitously, her words from earlier decades showed me the foundations of who I am, what I believe, and how I show up in my current life; her journal entries, scribbled with passion years ago, informed the origin story that helped me explain—and even forgive—myself.

Our journey—the one she began, the one I am completing—started out rather ragged and raw. Still, it has brought us to an older, perhaps wiser, version of ourself. Her words lent fresh insight to the origins of my beliefs. And with the passing of time, I could hold her dearly, seeing her with discernment, rather than judgment; I could witness and celebrate her strength, courage and fortitude; and I could reassure her of her sanity, the first step, I believe, toward our mutual healing.

gratitudes

Thank you for your special support...

This book was mined from decades of journals. To give thanks to those who offered support to me in its writing and publication requires that I give thanks to those who helped me live into-and-through its experiences, as well as those who helped me bring it to its printed form.

You unfathomably gifted me with many, many hours of your masterful attention, **Claire King** (PhD, CUNY tenured professor) delivering wonderfully nuanced edits—extensive, elegant, and for the infinite betterment of my work. I'm recalling fondly our luxurious, 45-minute discussion on whether to include that one comma.

You reliably and tirelessly helped raise my spirits—and my kids—too many times to recount, **Zarin & Dara Gandhi, Diana & Tom Maguire, Annie Roberts & Chuck Ziga, Karen & Gerry Pace,** and **Andrea Kostanecki**.

You generously read my pages—and occasionally read my mind—offering encouragement, perspective and love, **Diana Donnelley Smith, Barbara Geary Truan, Connie Pappas, Faith Curran Shelly, Kate Danielson Millar, Laurie Caswell Rosenberg, Avan Gandhi Bulger, Julia Shaw Henderson, Olga Kagan, Dan Kagan, Alex Schlater, Kristin Halvorsen, Mary Connaughty-Sullivan, Heidi Bement, Christie Greenleaf, Emily Kelting, Debra Pickett, Diane Caminins, Kate Vance, Lora Buono-Tyler, Annie Willcox, David Richards.**

You continue to play fearlessly—with me and everywhere—in the priority of presenced, mindful, aligned living **Abigail Stason, Sarah Carr, Margo Montgomery, Peggy Decker, the dedicated community of Hendricks.com, Kathlyn & Gay Hendricks, Hope Ross, Hugh Macready,** and **other members of the A Course in Miracles (ACIM) community**.

You held my hand—and the beating heart of this project—through the arduous details of development and publication, **Kelly Jenkins, Lisa Oliva, Alice-Anne Harwood Sherrill, Julia Maguire Henderson, Amy Lawless, Patti M. Hall, Martine Cameau, Denika Dutil, Gretchen Kelly, Jenn Grace, Brandi Lai, Bailly Morse, Angela Yeh,** and **Stephanie Larkin** and her team at **Red Penguin Books**.

You chose to walk the earth with me, dear sister, **Elizabeth Anne Guilday**, a gift that I hope continues in all my other lifetimes.

You remain my sightline in this lifetime, **Honor Sargent** and **Camden Sargent**, gifting me with your integrity and intelligence, your laughter and love.

Once upon a time, you agreed to be my husband, **John Sargent**, and even now, as my beautiful "was-band" in our revised version of happily-ever-after, I'm glad to call you my friend.

And you, **dear reader**, you spent your time with me in these pages. I am grateful.

Author & Contributors

Meet The Author, Molly Sargent

Molly Sargent has been writing poetry since the age of eight. She is a highly esteemed corporate facilitator and keynote speaker in sales enablement since 1985; she's an entrepreneur, serving Fortune 100 companies since 1997; and she's an avid student and practitioner of consciousness mindsets and skill sets since 2010, notable as the year her marriage began to unravel.

Scan to learn more about Sane Response & our team!

Special Thanks To:

Denika Dutil   Martine Cameau   Gretchen Kelly   Suzanne Uchytil

MollySargent.com

www.ingramcontent.com/pod-product-compliance
Lightning Source LLC
Chambersburg PA
CBHW061736070526
44585CB00024B/2696